In the Mind of a Writer

By Michael Mizzion Smith

In the Mind of a Writer

Copyright © 2017 by Michael Mizzion Smith

Cover Design by Adore Media Designs

Printed and bound in the United States of America

ISBN-13: 978-0-692-91144-0
Beyond Grace Publishing
Detroit, Michigan
www.beyondgracepublishing.com

This book is dedicated to Michael's Great Grandmother Johnnie Mae Smith & Great Grandfather Clifton A. Smith.

Special Note to My Biological Mother

I know we only knew each other for a short period of time, but your spirit of joy and happiness still resides in my heart. I was young when we met but I still remember your laugh when you use to watch your favorite television shows, as well as the sweet sound of your voice when you sang. I know you made a lot of decisions that people did not agree with. I have to say the best decision you ever made was to have me.
I thank you for that.

I Love you Rita E. Smith

Dedication

For my wife –For many years, I thought to publish my writings and share them with the world. However, without you I had no courage to do so. After we met, I began taking risks and started to face a lot of my professional fears. While others doubted me, you inspired me and encouraged me to keep pushing. From the bottom of my heart, I want to thank you for all your love, support and countless reinforcement. Before I found you, I had already accomplished a lot, but it wasn't until you came along that I started to reach for the stars.
I love you forever and always my 231.
Thank You, Chaetoya S. Smith

To my children –you three are amazing. Your bright smiles and wonderful spirits keep your father going. The love you all show is a blessing and means everything to me. I promise to always be there for you, and make life beautiful. I encourage you to go after your dreams as I am with this book. Thank you for being my beautiful children: London, Brooklyn & Houston Smith.

A Special Thanks

To a host of family and friends; Johnnie Mae Smith, Clifton A. Smith, John S. Smith Sr. & Jr., Renita McCoy-Smith, Roe Dayzon, Patricia Smith, Augustine Smith, Rachel Towns, Ira Towns, Clifton S. Smith, Jolena Jones, Gail Jones, Patrick Jones, Lanette E., Harren, Pastor Barry Randolph, David L. Green Sr., Pastor Janine Davis, Lynn & Cahlyn McCree, Katie Rhodes, Nique Love Rhodes, Leroy Harrison, Rodney Warren, Kurt Krug, Patricia Lanzon, Jenaye Libson, Tony Libson, Jezar Riches, Mr. & Mrs. Peace, Charnesha Thomas, Andre Hoskins and Deeyonna J. Gray

Table of Contents

FOREWORD

A twelve year boy wakes up with a strong hold on his heart, thinking to himself something is not right. He expresses his concerns to his cousin. The boy begins by saying, "I feel like a piece of me is missing." Just as he ends that statement, he hears a voice call him upstairs to the living room. After he is told to sit down, he hears the words, "Your Mom has passed." Falling to the ground, his heart was left on the floor.

He runs back downstairs entering his room, falls to his knees and screams, "Why me?" Just as he was heard by everyone in the house, his cousin enters the room saying, "I'm here for you." He replies, "I know, I just don't know what to do." His cousin consoles him and replies, "Be strong. You will find a way to cope." At that moment the twelve year boy picks up a pen and writes the words, "My Life" on a small piece of notebook paper. He then walks away from the paper and sits down on the couch. With tears falling down his face, he says to his cousin, "I think I know what I should do to cope, write my thoughts and express my hurt, my love, my joy, my pain, my life on paper."

In the Mind of a Writer

My Life

Life is full of Painful times,
But Love is the way to Healing.

Life is full of Growth,
But you cannot succeed without failing.

Life is full of Laughter,
But you cannot ignore the tears.

Life is full of Courage
But only if you face your fears.

My Life,
Is mine and I choose to live it.

My Life,
Is mine and I choose to give it – to Christ.

The Second Blessing

Oh, how she reminds me of happiness and joy. For every day that is to come, will be one that we collectively enjoy.

Her ten fingers and her ten toes, I count as I take in the greatness of God's design. I vow to protect everything about her starting with her mind.

To be an example that's my destiny.

To show her how she should be treated for all of her life.

To raise her to be Christ-like and to never lose her light.

Oh, how she reminds me of why I live and flourish.

To keep her in heaven's embrace and out of hell's furnace.

She is my Brooklyn, my baby born on 10/15.

She is my shining star.

She is my inspiration, she is my heart.

The Nuptial Grace

They say first comes *love*, then comes *marriage*, then comes
a baby in a baby carriage.

They say honeymoons bring *blessings* and ain't that the
truth. Finally I hear, *"it's a boy!"* and here comes you.

They say a father must groom his son to be a man.
Well from October fifth, twenty sixteen, I formed a plan
to give you the blueprint. You are so smart, so precious
and definitely heaven sent.

Your smile brightens up my world. You just got here,
already flirting with girls.

You are going be a hand full.
But you are father's son, I guess it's in our gene pool.

I will introduce you to respect and grace. Get you ready
for the chase, of your dreams and aspirations.

My son you will have a lot learn, and I will be in your
corner. I will always be your biggest supporter.

When you get older just give your father a call, you
might stumble but I will never let you fall.

MY LOVE FOR 231

Two times my soulmate,
Three times my dream,
One life to live, and finally I know, what true love
means.

Two times friend,
Three times my love,
One life to live, and I know our union is a blessing
from above.

Two times my truth,
Three times my heart,
One life to live, and you never let me fall apart.

Two times the grace.
Three times the joy.
One life live, and no distractions to avoid.

We are blessed, we gifted, we connected - we are one.

SOCIETY

This Society

Impatiently we wait for our wounds to heal. Soul clueless so we make a deal.

A temporary fix to our situations of unprecedented measures of pain. Impatiently we wait for a change.

Looking for a solution which we can't admit the problem. Alone we can't solve em.

There is a source of harmony and love. Navigate to this direction, it's above.

This Society

Blood shed like it's nothing when we all should treat it like it's something.

I know it may not affect you directly, but put yourself in their shoes. Now, look who's feeling the blues.

Nobody in this world is perfect. But it's our youth, they're worth it.

This Society

I shed a tear for every child we have lost at hands of hatred. Did we lose our patience?

A Reflection

I've indulged myself in reaching for the light. Walking away from the blade, similar to a knife.

I remember times where I could fight the fight and Love called me a knight.

I've grown in destruction. when construction were once my motives.

Days become longer in my dreams about joy. Displayed the qualities of a man, but the actions of a boy.

Merely surviving the battle because my armor wasn't on right. I could see it all, but the reflections of my thoughts blinded my sight.

Approaching the next level will take hard work. So I start with my belief that God is the answer, no more reason for the search...

Sanity

In the mind of the lost, their sanity is the cost. Wanting to stand strong as a tree. So rooted, yet so free. Decisions have consequences and life has an end. But the truth that lies within, is where life begins. Yet it is a sin to doubt positive outcomes to situations of impurity and challenge. Manage your thoughts and plan your actions. Ambition is just a fraction of the qualities required to succeed at interaction with your counterparts. Your heart is fragile but oh so special, and to your travels take them seriously because life is a gift. Don't take it lightly, you have been provided with all the necessary tools to align yourself with happiness. Bringing forth a smile, and this time it won't just last a little while.

Spoken Expressions

I've heard life ain't no crystal stare. And we are the hope of the slaves. There's been the reference of a dream deferred. A million times in my thoughts are where these lines have occurred. I've read true love is defined by your capability to be vulnerable. Consistency is linked with what's right. When you indulge into the darkness, you have no desire for the light. People have said there is no gain, without the existence of pain. You're designed to accept what you hear when you are not open to change. I'm perfectly fine with the storm because sometimes it has to rain.

Suicidal He

*T*ears fall from this man's face, for only happiness was among the chase. And sadness filled his whole being; he had been surrounded by degradation and pain. Whips and chains, of society, swung against his flesh and his whole life had become a mess. He had no direction because the street signs were missing. He had no idea what he should hear because he wasn't listening. A man pushing everyone away, and saying he could end it all any day. No more worries and no need for change. He had beaten his own destiny out of range.

Laughing to hold back from crying, that was who he was. Love, seemed to be so far from his heart, because he was willing to tear those who cared completely apart. He got a text on his phone saying, *please call me*. He ignored it began to leave, leave his body, leave his mind. No control of time, the seconds started moving slower, and slower, and slower... *Knock, Knock*... open the door, the voice suddenly pressed to say. The Man replied with saying, *no way*. He proceeded to open the chamber and loaded it heavy, for he had found himself ready to depart forever. For his soul felt like the stormy weather, and all he could see was death.

Suicidal Not He, but Me.

You Say

You say your dreams are far passed the
heights in the sky. And life is in space, so
you're reaching for the stars.
You say I'm pushing against this brick wall, but
you can't knock it down because you ain't
standing tall.
You say, how can I break this cold, when I
can't weather the storm. You'll be surprised
how faith can keep you warm.
You walk with a stumble because you didn't
learn how to crawl.
You say you ready for a war but life is a brawl.
And that ain't all; you really want to know why
life is so hard.
Everything is falling around you and you fold
your cards. Well, just around the corner is
relief.
A little bit of patience and a whole lot of belief.
Now you're swimming through life's ocean to
the reef

Little Angel of Mine

Eighteenth of March, and you were born.

Eighteenth of March, and our bond was formed.

Beautiful eyes, and a head full of hair.

Precious and wonderful, nothing else could compare.

You are pure in nature, and I'm glad GOD decided to share you on this earth.

I have been so changed, and reformed since your birth.

Six years later, and oh how you have grown. As long as I got you, my dear, I will never be alone.

Your intelligence surprises, me every time we sit and color, and you articulate your thoughts.

I've been captured by your innocence, so with that, I don't mind being caught.

We've have looked in the mirror, smiling exactly the same way. I love you, and cherish you, each and every day.

You are my joy in my sadness. You are my light in my darkness.

You are my love when I'm surrounded by hate. You came into this world just in time, so your presence will never be late.

You are my daughter, so remember you will always be great.

Lonely Bench

The clouds had falling tears.
Well, I've been rained on for many years.
From picnics to food and stains.
A King left from a lucky card game.
Sticky bubble gum, left on me.
Sweet stuff left, for the bumble-bees.
Barbeque ribs, left to toast.
For the possums and raccoons to roast.
Dirt beneath, my flat feet.
For many years my wooden legs, were too weak.
Holding on to my strength, while the wind blows.
Taking care of my weight, not letting go.
The clouds had falling tears.
Well I've been snowed on for many years.
From my frozen seat, to my frozen back.
The ice so thick, not a creature could relax.
Surrounding my body, nothing in sight.
Not a soul, but a lonely quiet night.
The clouds had falling tears.
Like the trees had falling leaves every year.
A mixture of a rainbow, colors covered the ground.
The same beauty, where I lie, covered the town.
Piles of their existence, begin to fade.
When the cold winter brings, about the freezing shade.
Yet when the cold seems, to disappear.
The bright and joyful sun, dreams to appear.
No longer will the clouds, have falling tears.
Because the sun, has made its presence known,
Again this year.

FROM LUST TO LOVE

Can hardly breathe. Thoughts and feelings harden by the moments full of uncertainty. Lust was the thing hurting me. Had begun to walk, but instantly fell. Steps suddenly became louder and louder, and seem to never have an ending. Deep hole in his soul, and not a thing to hold on to. Not a smile, not fantasy, not even one truth. Pain is not the right phrase to describe his emotion. He has been struck by lust's unforgiving potion. Change is not an option, he has tried a million times. His attempts weakened by his lack of confidence, and he went over his lines one million more times. Now he is stuck in a pool of failing himself. Surrounded by reasons to continue life, he decided to renew what he had been given. For so long he had kept hidden his most guarded inner thoughts. For a man like this really fought to be accepted by lust, with lust, and for lust.

Funny thing is he had not truly found who he was, blocked by memories of a drama filled childhood, constantly blaming everyone else. Although he had no part in some of his experiences of being "damaged", he has the chance to overcome it. He prayed to the heavens above for guidance when his heart was removed, and replaced with a wall. One day, he thought, I will stand tall. Overcome it all, and be brand new. But who knew it would take that same lust to make him see he had the main ingredient within himself to change everything. Everywhere and every time he doubted his potential. It was essential to his development to understand he had not reached his plateau.

This guy would compare his pain to weights on his chest. He said that there would be no rest until he clear all the mess from his life. That's when he found Love and he asked her to be his wife.

Grandma Smith

Don't let there be tears,
Just appreciation and joy, down in our souls.
The love she shared, will not grow old.
Taught us all how to fight.
She sure would tell you, if you were wrong or right.
She lived her life, among true love.
She was truly this family's gift, from above.
So let this moment, bring us together.
For she will be with us, forever.

Great Granddaddy

Strong and stable, like a bark of a tree.

Longevity displayed, but now set free.

A time of grief, but yet a celebration of life shared.

Love and joy, never to be compared.

A steadfast individual, but with his partner —what a pair.

Strength and conviction, all well intention to educate.

And leave a legacy to be remembered, from generation to generation.

A great man, who seems to be the blueprint for the family plan.

Yet, with the Lord, he will stand, in the hearts and minds of those connected to earth.

But I know, we all will acknowledge his worth.

Rose

Divine like a glass of wine, over time even age develops so fine. The reflection of undeniable appeal. Oh, how this flower makes me feel. Refreshing and strengthens the desire I have, to take one more sniff of the petals of such a sexy, and genuine symbol of affection.

Draws a smile in the most awkward times, the motivation for about a million more lines, and don't have to rhyme. A rose whose beauty could resemble that the taste of a peach. I'm so glad you're not out of reach. I'll let your example of maturity and intelligence teach.

Red, White and Pink, I just love that hair on your head. Your eyes that bring a surprisingly limelight and even when you blink, my heart sinks at the thought of a rose that stands out being mine. So bloom continuously, as you shine.

CRYSTAL CLEAR

Focus, tune in, listen up, right here, right now.

Impression, opinion, your thoughts, please.

Your concern, your best wishes, your love for thee.

Only once, this one time, what is it you see.

The questions, I'm asking you, one would like to know.

On the move, forward we go.

So smooth, so suave, let your words just flow.

Present, today, this hour, a rose, a carnation, a flower.

You'll learn, you'll see the lesson, you'll be educated.

So many ways to speak of, say, make it crystal clear.

Sitting in a Room

Sitting in a room, enclosed by limitations. Formed by the laws of a basic foundation. Planted by the same individuals who had great expectations, for the room I'm sitting in.

Staring out a window wondering if I should let the aroma and outside wind come right on in. Just like every common thing a person may have use for was invented by a black man or black woman. Can things so different blend in together? Well, if I never stop sitting in this room, I will never know. Leaving my comfort zone is that the way to go?

Letting confused thoughts continue to flow, and stuck in a society that is all show. But remembering to share the knowledge and continue the wealth, for only when we as a people realize that what we believe is our only true help. So if it's love, it could be lust in disguise. Instead of feeling butterflies, you're surrounded by flies, and when your high comes down, your determination dies. But if it's surrounded by true faith and not referring to fate. Then the window I'm looking out of, is a tunnel to the gate. By the time I look at the clock, it's a quarter to eight and now knowing that my heart's contentment, was the bait for that of a force of destruction.

Therefore, taking instruction to look deeper into the mirror with a reflection of myself, life feeling distant, grasp it with a deep desire, for now being consecrated in relaxation, concentrated on my destination. Eternity.

HERE I AM

Thoughts make the pain larger, but thoughts also make the pain go away. What I face here is a paradox, by a situation I created with the image of happiness in mind. Yet, it seems I have to work so damn hard to make it succeed. Indeed I love the journey life has got me going through. But who knew about the threshold of trials and tribulations. This one time could there be no stipulation, on my destination of accomplishment. Just once, I wish my joy didn't need adjustment, but to be a testament for others to see. For me, the road is everlasting, yet it seems I'm always passing signs for road repairs. Who cares if I've tried? If I've failed then there is no tomorrow, just dark clouds and sorrow, being drowned in my lost ways to deal with it. I feel sick every time I cannot finish it, and by it, I mean the subject of my ambition. Must I mention the hours of defeat I've taken? The moments where my whole world was shaken, yet now I'm breaking through with things to be happy for, that's right opportunity is at my door, it's time to answer.

HERE I AM

Emotions

Heart's throbbing, every beat harder than a drum. Sweat running down your face, relief none. Pulse is getting faster, at a pace that's unbearable.

Thoughts are deeply softened by the occurrence of joy, experienced by your moments of life. Gifts from heaven are given daily but only appreciated when acknowledged. Is that how society wants to be remembered? Beauty, a mere reflection of existence on this earth, like childbirth, unforgettable and comparable to nothing, yet death is something that affects us all. Pride stands tall and hears no evil.

Links components of love to connect grace with mercy which is given to last forever and never gives up on faith for it lasts as long as you believe. A laugh, for every moment you share self with a friend. A tear, for every moment you see this side of the grass and trees still have leaves that will grow.

Words flow continuously through the mind, and prayer is divine and ages very well. Life has an aroma of comfort to mend any broken soul. An angry face, for the moments of disappointment but release comes by a commitment to the resolution.

There is...

There is a black light hanging above my dresser, in my bedroom. Wondering if the joy I'm hoping for, will come soon. There is a reflection of the night light, you know the moon. Near the old clock in my living room. There is a sound I hear late at night, when sleep is supposed to be my best friend. There is a picture of my favorite actress, on my night stand. If I could get her, that would make me a man.

These are thoughts of a confused teenage boy, who wants to become a man. Yet, he has not discovered the story of the resurrection, the guarantee of protection, the division of life's selection. Yet, he has found the deception of the male erection. But hold all emotion, for that's just the beginning.

There is a crowd with all the wrong intentions; you know the ones your child fails to mention. There is a quote –unquote, popular way to handled things, blinded by all the diamond chains and earrings. They say life is what you make it. Not dedicated to God, then the devil shall take it.

There is confusion to every situation, but patience is the key to happiness. Yet, diligently seeking equals righteousness. Holy is not a risk, it's a gift. So realizing whose winning, can put evil to its' ending.

OUR TROOPS

WE fight for a cause. Please don't tell me that.

Liberation of rights, that's why we fight. To live every day out of the darkness, and into the light. The pursuit of happiness is guaranteed, but pain and degradation dwell inside of dreams –of the men and women who want to come home. What do I mean?

Blood being shed over greed and revenge, to a cause that once was just, but now undefined. Land mines, bombs, and gun powder in the air, on the ground and in the memories of those who give the sacrifice of life to continue its existence.

For 9/11 was the beginning of the fall, the cause that has been called, "Liberation Iraq" more than one simple attack, but now a plaque of death and sorrow. For we all wish just today, not tomorrow, that we see those faces that made us smile. Strength for a mile and appear in the U S of A. any day. President of our great country, making souls and hearts surround with warmth to hear, "They're coming home".

Yet, we sit at the throne of Christ, submit our prayers for mercy to endure throughout the times we have come to face. We want joy and love to accompany this place and freedom to reign without disgrace.

The _Truth_ is more than what's right.

The life we choose to live not only affects us, but those we care about the most. The heart is a vessel strong in construction, but weak by our emotions. We believe in governmental hypocrisy and conspiracy, when we fail to believe in expediential miracles and faith. We challenge the concepts our four fathers presented as our precedent foundations. We stand now alone in our war for morality and stability to dream pass the sky's limits. We limited ourselves to levels of comfort, when we are far more than the status quo. We are children of a King, one whose grace is not measurable. The mercy he has brought to our existence is breathtaking. And if you catch yourself shaking in grief, just remember that it starts with your belief in Love –not one with conditions but one with extraordinary results. Push through the pain you so often feel and know that salvation is real. Guilt for what you have experience in this life, but you must give reverence to the light that shines from Christ. To understand who you truly are, you must humble yourself. Realizing its okay to be human and ask for help. Do not depreciate the value of your gifts, with the failure to utilize them when the opportunity reveals itself. Knowledge is the key to preserving your wealth. Not just monetary, but the soul that God designed in his image. The perception of destruction in your eyes is where you lose focus on life's ultimate prize, and the strength in your spirit is where the voice of reason makes itself loud enough for you to hear it. You say you have been given too much bare, and your footsteps are getting longer in the sand. But stop looking for his hand and be in search for his face, let us stop all this division and become the Lord's human race.

Empty Void

Left my heart in the empty void I called my life, and I stood alone away from the heights of Christ. I change all my thoughts so they would match my pain. I remained the same, because I didn't want to change. Mental capacity was full, with the infection. I put my guard down, didn't want his protection. Propaganda in my life, like an election. Glass cracked from the hatred, of my reflection. Silence in the room, I must be MIC checking. No forensics on my problems, cause I wasn't detecting. The first step is to admit there was something there, pollution in my lungs cutting off my air. Break all the rules, no one said life was fair. Kept standing because the world, had no more chairs. I invested in the wrong stock, lost my all shares. Society is a beast, better be aware. I've broken shackles that I once use to wear. Got God in my life, now nothing compares. Paying forward the blessings, that I was provided. So much joy inside of me, I could not hide it. I've reached a place in my journey, where I had to take action. No more stagger movements, or slowed reaction. My dreams had just become a minor fraction, from all the additives in my life, and the countless subtraction. The people I had to let go of, to get where I need to be. I didn't understand my purpose, because I lost my understanding of me.

Storm

A pounding sound against the window seal. A clinging rattle that won't stop in the late hours of the night. Reverb voices and hollow clapping with screaming thunder that scares the people next door.

Thrusting wind, water smashing towards the siding on that brick house on the corner. No picket white fences to gaze at on a summer day.

Banging noises keep you awake. Glass falls two feet and breaks. A million pieces become fragments of the whole orchestra of chaos.

Ringing in your ears is peaceful and full of grace. Suddenly the storm becomes music.

Sorrow

The pain that has been caused, feels like a million mountains crashing down on life. The strife that happens to be stabbing us, feels like the sharpest knife. There has been murder, committed against that thing we call a smile. The stripes we face, will last longer than a mile. The world's condition tells so many stories, of the horror society has created. The actions that have taken place are hated, and the future is not for sure. But what is standing at the door where mankind wears it's heart on its sleeve, evil has taken our oxygen, so now we can't breathe.

There has become a stigma, where what our leaders tell us we can't believe. The truth is without love, our goals and aspirations we cannot achieve. So open our wounds, and let them bleed. The one thing we forget is that God hears our prayers, so let's collectively bend down to our knees.

Not reaching our potential, because we have defeated ourselves with our decisions. Decisions that press against God's good will. So now we are stuck on this hill of regret. I bet we could've been somewhere greater than this moment right here. So it's time to let God wipe our generational tear.

Breathe In, Breathe Out

F uzzy visions of perfection, lacking certainty of who I am. Scratching my head, trying to figure it out if my computer is running out of ram. Upgrade to a new version, so that I keep up with the times. Paper has a lot of information, and there are still a few lines. Composition of music, playing in sequences not even designed yet. I have made changes, to myself without regret. The days ahead hold so much promise, so listen to this. Be faithful to the cause and where you decide to take a pause, smell the future, and breathe in… breathe out.

Inspiration

The tree branches blow in the wind, and there is a fire in the sky.
The sun shines so bright on this day.
Days prior to this one were so dark and cold.
Water freezes over from the frosty mornings of winter pain.
Rain melts away the afflictions of the people.
Freedom is a privilege that we take for granted.
My pathway is straight but with life's obstacles, it appears slanted.
I assure you though, with God I'm firmly planted.

THE MIRACLE LIES
BETWEEN THE LINES.

HE WAS BORN INTO POVERTY AND MISFORTUNE.
BUT HIS DESTINY WASN'T FAR FROM DESIGNED.

HE WAS BORN INTO BROKEN PROMISES AND PAIN.
BUT HIS LIFE WAS SURE TO CHANGE.

HE WAS BORN INTO UNCERTAINTY AND QUESTION.
BUT HIS REACH FOR SUCCESS WOULD INCREASE OVER TIME.

HE LEARNED QUICKLY THE POWER OF ONE'S MIND.
HE WAS BORN INTO POTENTIAL WITH WIDE OPEN RANGE.

AND HIS BOOK WAS TO WRITTEN DOWN TO THE LAST PAGE.
SO HE TOOK THE NECESSARY STEPS TO BE FRONT STAGE.

About the Author

Michael Mizzion Smith born Michael Steven Smith in 1984, is best known for his work in the independent film industry. Born and raised in Detroit, Michael displayed signs of creativity early on. Throughout the years, his passion for the arts spread into music and film production, photography, and writing.

Mr. Smith holds a Bachelor's degree in Business Administration and Master's degree in Digital Marketing. He wrote this book to express his thoughts about current events, issues that affect society, and to share his heartfelt memories with the reading audience.

Michael is best described as a gentleman, who is a devoted husband and loving father to his three children. If you were to meet him, he would say his family is his life's biggest achievements in life and London, Brooklyn, and Houston, his leading inspirations.

Despite ignoring the signs of mental illness, Michael Mizzion Smith faced a time where he thought life was not worth living. But God saw a purpose that needed to be fulfilled in his life and kept him here on earth.

After a fail suicide attempt during a very low point his life, he began to use his God-given gifts to change other people's lives. Through writing, photography and film, Michael Mizzion Smith has been a blessing to so many.

He is a person who has always been known best for expressing himself through his writings. You will learn so much about his heart and soul within this book of poetry.

www.ingramcontent.com/pod-product-compliance
Lightning Source LLC
Chambersburg PA
CBHW072039060426
42449CB00010BA/2348